The Resignation
of Nixon

THE RESIGNATION OF NIXON

In the early morning hours of June 17, 1972, five intruders, carrying electronic equipment, were caught in the Democratic National Committee offices in the Watergate building in Washington, D.C. From this seemingly insignificant beginning ever-enlarging revelations of political intrigue and illegal activities spread through the Republican administration of Richard Nixon until what came to be known as the Watergate Affair culminated in the first resignation of an American President.

PRINCIPALS

WATERGATE, a place not a person: a modernistic office-apartment complex in Washington, D.C., in which was launched the most extensive political scandal in American history

*Among those whose careers
were damaged or destroyed
by Watergate exposures:*

RICHARD MILHOUS NIXON, thirty-seventh President of the United States, 1969–74

JOHN N. MITCHELL, former U.S. Attorney General; former director, Committee for the Re-election of the President (CRP)

MAURICE H. STANS, former Secretary of Commerce; former chairman, Finance Committee to Re-elect the President (FCRP)

JEB STUART MAGRUDER, former special assistant to the President, former deputy director of CRP, who confessed he had committed perjury when testifying about Watergate

PATRICK L. GRAY, whom Nixon appointed acting director of the FBI after the death of J. Edgar Hoover

H. R. HALDEMAN, White House chief of staff during the Nixon administration

JOHN D. EHRLICHMAN, former chief domestic affairs adviser to Nixon

JOHN W. DEAN III, former counsel to Nixon, the first to implicate the President in Watergate

CHARLES W. COLSON, former special counsel to Nixon, involved in a number of questionable White House activities

DONALD H. SEGRETTI, who conducted espionage and sabotage, known as "Dirty Tricks," against the Democrats

THE FIVE WATERGATE BURGLARS: James W. McCord, Eugenio E. Martinez, Virgilio Gonzales, Bernard L. Barker, Frank Sturgis; their two fellow conspirators: E. HOWARD HUNT, former CIA agent and former White House consultant, and G. GORDON LIDDY, former White House aide, former counsel of CRP, and staff member of FCRP

*Among those who sought
truth and justice on Watergate
and related scandals:*

JUDGE JOHN J. SIRICA, who, as chief judge of the U.S. District Court, Washington, D.C., presided over the original trial of the five Watergate burglars, plus Hunt and Liddy, and later over the Watergate conspiracy trial of Mitchell and others

SENATOR SAM J. ERVIN, North Carolina Democrat, chairman of the Senate Select Committee on Presidential Campaign Activities, known as the Watergate Committee

ARCHIBALD COX, Watergate Special Prosecutor until October 20, 1973, who refused to curtail his investigations even when the trail led to the White House

ELLIOT L. RICHARDSON, former Attorney General, who resigned rather than comply with White House instructions to fire Prosecutor Cox

LEON JAWORSKI, a Houston lawyer, successor to Archibald Cox as Watergate Special Prosecutor

REPRESENTATIVE PETER W. RODINO, JR., New Jersey Democrat, chairman of the House Judiciary Committee, which conducted proceedings to consider the impeachment of President Nixon

WARREN E. BURGER, Chief Justice of the U.S. Supreme Court, which found unanimously that the President of the United States had no right to withhold evidence in criminal proceedings

A FOCUS BOOK

The Resignation of Nixon

*A Discredited President
Gives Up the
Nation's Highest Office*

by Robin McKown

FRANKLIN WATTS | NEW YORK | LONDON

The author and publisher wish to acknowledge the helpful suggestions of Theodore Shabad.

Cover by Ginger Giles

Photographs courtesy of: United Press International: pages 4, 8, 14, 24, 29, 53, 59, 68; Wide World Photos: pages 17, 45; Franklin Watts, Inc.: facing page 1.

Library of Congress Cataloging in Publication Data

McKown, Robin.
    The resignation of Nixon.

    (A Focus book)
    Bibliography: p.
    Includes index.
    SUMMARY: Traces the events that led to the first resignation of a President in United States history.
    1. Watergate Affair, 1972–   —Juvenile literature. [1. Watergate Affair, 1972] I. Title.
E860.M38   973.924′092′4   75-8538
ISBN 0-531-01092-9

Contents

For Betty and Ted Clark

Other Books
by Robin McKown

Nonfiction

The Colonial Conquest of Africa
The Republic of Zaïre
The Execution of Maximilian
Opium War in China
Lumumba
Nkrumah
Crisis in South Africa
The Image of Puerto Rico
The Congo, River of Mystery
Heroic Nurses
The World of Mary Cassatt
Mark Twain

Fiction

The Boy Who Woke Up in Madagascar
Girl of Madagascar
Rakoto and the Drongo Bird
The Ordeal of Anne Devlin
Janine
Patriot of the Underground

*The White House, official residence of
the President of the United States*

A Unique Event

*"America is in trouble today
not because her people
have failed but because
her leaders have failed."*

*Richard Nixon to
his cheering Republican
convention delegates in
Miami, August 1968*

On August 8, 1974, Richard Milhous Nixon, age sixty-one, addressed the American people over nationwide television from the Oval Office of the White House to announce that he was resigning his post as President of the United States, effective the following day.

Nixon, who had won his second term in 1972 by a record victory (60.8 percent of the popular vote and 97 percent of the electoral vote), was the first President in American history to resign. He was the second American President against whom impeachment proceedings had been brought. The other was President Andrew Johnson, who had been acquitted of the impeachment charges by the Senate and allowed to finish his term in office. Nixon resigned before impeachment charges came to a vote in the full House.

The scandals that led to Nixon's resignation, formed of an entangled mesh of actions and events, will most likely go down in history as the Watergate Affair. These scandals were the biggest and most extensive ever to hit the country, not excepting the notorious Teapot Dome Scandal during President Warren Harding's administration.

Mixed reactions greeted Nixon's resignation announcement. In front of the White House a group of Nixon supporters gathered, holding aloft American flags and placards. One of them read, "We love you, Mr. President." On the other hand, Harvard students danced in the streets of Cambridge. In an art gallery in black Harlem, someone called, "Bring out the champagne!" In Peoria, Illinois, the heart of middle-class America, Mayor Richard Carver commented, "If he had just said 'I'm sorry,' I would have felt a little better about it."

"The agony is over," said GOP Senator Robert P. Griffin of Michigan. "The long dark night is over," said Democratic Senator Frank Church of Idaho. "The country has been on the verge of a nervous breakdown long enough," declared Senate Republican Leader Hugh Scott of Pennsylvania. Senator George McGovern, Nixon's opponent in the 1972 elections, said, "The loss of the presidency is the worst penalty, the harshest punishment that could be imposed."

"Our long national nightmare is over," said Gerald Ford, the first President in American history to gain his post without being elected on a national ticket.

The Band
of Burglars

"Nobody acts innocent."

Assistant Attorney General
Henry Petersen

In the predawn hours of June 17, 1972, five men broke into the Democratic National Committee headquarters on the sixth floor of an office building in Watergate, an ultramodern complex of buildings facing the Potomac River in Washington, D.C. Three plainclothesmen, alerted by the young security guard, Frank Wills, found them crouching behind a desk. At police headquarters the five were booked and searched. They were loaded down with a telephone bugging device, a walkie-talkie, two cameras, forty rolls of unexposed film, tear-gas pens, and over $1,200 in cash among them, mostly in $100 bills.

Four of the prisoners came from Miami—Eugenio R. Martinez, Virgilio Gonzales, both Cuban exiles, Bernard L. Barker, who was part Cuban, and Frank Sturgis, a former marine and Air Force pilot. They had all been involved in the unsuccessful Bay of Pigs invasion of Cuba, sponsored by the Central Intelligence Agency (CIA). The fifth prisoner, James W. McCord, Jr., had been with the CIA for twenty years as an electronic surveillance technician. He was at the time of his arrest employed as director of security for the Committee for the Re-election of the President, a Nixon campaign organization.

Within a week after the arrest Democratic Chairman Lawrence O'Brien announced a $1 million civil suit against the Committee for the Re-election of the President, charging that there

Watergate is a "city within a city" that includes apartments,
a huge office building, a hotel, a shopping center, and
the John F. Kennedy Center for the Performing Arts (right).

was a "clear developing line" from the Watergate break-in to the White House. The suit would be settled on the date of Nixon's resignation by a payment of $775,000 to the Democrats. At the time, however, O'Brien's charges were generally dismissed as the usual campaign rhetoric.

Yet before the end of June, Federal Bureau of Investigation (FBI) agents had tracked down three more Watergate conspirators whose backgrounds showed an even closer link with the Nixon administration—Alfred Baldwin, who, equipped with a walkie-talkie, had been on watch the night of the break-in, and George Gordon Liddy and E. Howard Hunt, who were also keeping check on the burglars. In rooms they had rented in the Watergate Hotel, the FBI found thirty-two more new $100 bills.

Gordon Liddy was a lawyer, a former prosecuting attorney, an unsuccessful candidate for congressman, and, like James McCord, worked for the Committee for the Re-election of the President. Howard Hunt was a CIA veteran whose service dated back to the CIA involvement in the overthrow of the Arbenz government in Guatemala in 1954. He had also helped plan the Bay of Pigs; Cubans in Miami knew him as "Eduardo," one of several aliases. He had been working for the White House as consultant on security matters.

Alfred Baldwin had been bodyguard for Martha Mitchell, wife of the re-election campaign director and former Attorney General John Mitchell. To avoid prosecution, Baldwin was willing to talk. From him the prosecution would learn that the same men had broken into the Democratic headquarters two weeks before and had bugged the telephones of O'Brien and a colleague, Spencer Oliver. From a motel room across the street, Baldwin had transcribed their calls, giving his transcription to McCord. The second break-in, on June 17, was made to repair the tap on O'Brien's phone, Baldwin said.

Assistant U.S. Attorney Earl J. Silbert was assigned to the

case. From the outset he met with frustration. An FBI man in Miami learned that $114,000 had been deposited in defendant Bernard Barker's bank account in the form of a $25,000 cashier's check, made payable to Kenneth Dahlberg, and four checks totaling $89,000 issued by a Mexican bank. Sending money from the States to another country to hide its source is called "laundering." The FBI had the means to trace it, but this was not done. Not the FBI but two *Washington Post* reporters, Carl Bernstein and Bob Woodward, discovered that Kenneth Dahlberg was head of a Minneapolis branch of the Nixon campaign committee. Prosecutor Silbert was advised by Assistant Attorney General Henry Petersen to limit his investigation only to Watergate. It was not to be "a fishing expedition" to embarrass the President.

It would later be revealed that the Watergate break-in was only one of numerous illegal or highly unethical actions sponsored by the Nixon administration.

At the outset of the 1972 election campaign, Nixon had set up two campaign committees: the Committee for the Re-election of the President, known as CRP, and the Finance Committee for the Re-election of the President, known as FCRP. Former Attorney General John Mitchell became director of the CRP in February 1972. The chairman of FCRP, responsible for raising campaign funds, was former Secretary of Commerce Maurice Stans. The two committees worked closely together and shared the same offices. Their ties with the White House were equally close.

By April 1972, seventeen former White House or administration employees were among the twenty-three senior CRP or FCRP staff members. The FCRP treasurer, Hugh W. Sloan, was formerly staff assistant to Nixon. Frederick C. LaRue, Mississippi oil heir, had served as a Nixon aide without pay before being transferred to CRP. The CRP scheduling director, Herbert L. Porter, had worked at the White House. Jeb Stuart Magruder, deputy director of CRP, had also been with the White House. His job was improving the President's image with the press. The official liaison officer between the committees and the White House was Gordon Creighton Strachan, who reported all CRP and FCRP matters directly to H. R. (Bob) Haldeman, Nixon's chief of staff.

The National Republican Party had a certain resentment against CRP and FCRP. It felt the two committees represented a Nixon effort to siphon off big campaign contributions for himself to the detriment of lesser Republican candidates. Before the campaign ended, more than $50 million, a record-breaking amount, would be collected to insure the re-election of Richard Nixon. Later testimony would reveal the strong pressure and incentives used on individuals and corporations to extract large, and often illegal, contributions.

Not untypical of what was going on was a pre-Watergate scandal involving the powerful International Telephone and Telegraph Company, exposed first by investigative reporter Jack Anderson. Anderson produced evidence that ITT had offered a $400,000 contribution to the Nixon campaign committee in return for the assurance that the Justice Department would drop its objections to an ITT merger with the Hartford Fire Insurance Company. In Senate hearings, John Mitchell, who was still Attorney General and thus head of the Justice Department, denied any knowledge of the deal.

Gordon Liddy was sent from the White House to CRP to work at "intelligence gathering." Jeb Magruder and former White House counsel John Wesley Dean III have both vividly described the scene in John Mitchell's office when Liddy, equipped with large charts, submitted "a million-dollar espionage plan." The plan included mugging squads, sabotage, break-ins, electronic surveillance, wiretapping, call girls to blackmail

Former Attorney General John N. Mitchell as he testified in March 1972 before the Senate Judiciary Committee investigating the ITT merger

leading Democrats, kidnappers to inject radicals with drugs and transport them to Mexico.

According to the testimony of the others present, Mitchell, whom Nixon had once called "the leader of our fight against crime and lawlessness," said, "Why don't you tone it down a little, Gordon?" Liddy submitted a revised plan in February, which was also turned down. In late March 1972, under pressure from the White House, Mitchell, according to Magruder's testimony, approved Liddy's second downward revision of the plan. It now cost $250,000, excluded call girls and kidnapping and mugging, but gave high priority to the break-in and bugging of the Democratic campaign headquarters at the Watergate.

This was the genesis of the two Watergate break-ins, the first when wiretaps were successfully placed, and the second when the men were caught. The telephone conversations of the Democrats, transcribed by Alfred Baldwin, reportedly reached Mitchell's desk—after Liddy had them typed up on stationery marked "Gemstone." Mitchell found them worthless. According to Jeb Magruder, Mitchell had authorized the whole scheme only because of White House pressure.

The Senate Watergate Report, published two years later, commented on the attitude found in the White House in this pre-Watergate period:

> *The evidence shows that, from the early days of the present Administration, the power of the President was viewed by some in the White House as almost without limit. Especially if national or internal security was invoked, even criminal laws were considered subordinate to presidential decision or strategy.*

Some eighty persons were on the White House staff, of whom only a handful had the President's confidence. Bob Haldeman, Nixon's chief of staff, was, next to Nixon, the most powerful man in the White House. Others in the administration and Congress, cabinet ministers and senators included, had to go through Haldeman to see Nixon. Haldeman fully shared Nixon's political beliefs and attitudes and they worked closely together in developing policies that many considered repressive toward ideological opponents. When Haldeman gave orders to other White House aides, they had reason to believe the orders came from Nixon and must be obeyed without question.

Second, after Haldeman, in the White House hierarchy was John Ehrlichman, chief domestic adviser, who also gave orders in the name of the President. John Dean, counsel to the President, was next in line. He was often given distasteful tasks which Haldeman and Ehrlichman did not want to do themselves. To carry on what amounted to an underground war against the opposition, Dwight L. Chapin, appointments secretary to the President, hired Donald Segretti to harass the Democrats with "Dirty Tricks"; Egil Krogh headed a group called "the Plumbers," whose job was theoretically to stop leaks of top-secret documents; Charles W. Colson, special counsel to the President, sponsored numerous unsavory projects, including a forged cable implicating President Kennedy in the murder of President Diem in South Vietnam.

The misdeeds at CRP, FCRP, and the White House were all top secret when Prosecutor Silbert began to investigate and build his case against the "Watergate Seven." Of numerous witnesses he questioned, an estimated twenty were later revealed to have lied or withheld information. Jeb Magruder, who later admitted to lying, testified that Gordon Liddy had been given $100,000 to send ten agents onto college campuses and infiltrate radical groups—his explanation of the money found on the Watergate burglars. According to Magruder, Liddy had acted on his own in "bugging" Watergate. FCRP treasurer, young Hugh

Sloan, refused to commit perjury about the cash he had given to Liddy, quitting his job instead. He became one of the few heroes of Watergate.

Indictments against the seven men were brought in September. U.S. District Court Chief Judge John J. Sirica assigned the case to himself. He had the reputation of being tough and opinionated but of stainless integrity. The trial opened on January 10, 1973. Prosecutor Silbert based his charges on Magruder's unlikely story that the men were acting on their own. Howard Hunt and the four Miami men pleaded guilty.

Angrily, Sirica asked defendant Barker how he got all "those hundred-dollar bills floating around like coupons." Barker said the money was sent him in the mail in a blank envelope. The others said nothing. James McCord and Gordon Liddy also kept silent during their trial. They were pronounced guilty on January 30—ten days after Nixon's spectacular inauguration.

The sentencing of the defendants was held off until March 23. Judge Sirica would give them all heavy provisional sentences and fines. But the most sensational event of this second part of the trial was an astonishing letter Judge Sirica read to the court from defendant James McCord, the first of the seven to break the eight months of silence.

Political pressure had been applied to the defendants to plead guilty and keep silent, McCord wrote. Perjury had occurred during the trial; others involved in Watergate had not been identified. He asked for permission to talk privately with the judge, since he did not feel confident of talking with an FBI agent or with a grand jury whose U.S. attorneys worked for the Department of Justice.

The FBI? The Department of Justice? How could they be distrusted? The implications were staggering. The reporters in the courtroom rushed out to call their papers.

A Rough Journey
from Yorba Linda to
the White House

*"We come from typical everyday
American families that have
had to work for what they got
out of life, but always knew
there was unlimited opportunity."*

Pat Nixon

The town of Yorba Linda, where Richard Milhous Nixon was born on January 9, 1913, is some twenty-five miles inland from Los Angeles. In 1922 the family moved about fifteen miles closer to Los Angeles, to Whittier. Both Richard's parents were Quakers. His father ran one of the early gas stations and turned an old Quaker meetinghouse into a grocery store.

As a schoolboy, Richard was reportedly bright, serious, hard-working, shy. In high school he won several competitions for debating. He attended Whittier College, went on to Duke University's law school, and, after passing his California bar examinations, joined a law firm in Whittier. His chief diversion was acting in the Little Theatre, where he met his future wife, Thelma Catherine (Pat) Ryan.

When the Second World War broke out, Nixon worked in the Office of Price Administration in Washington, but he was unhappy amidst the New Dealers of the Roosevelt administration. His request for a Navy commission granted, in May 1943,

Lieutenant Nixon shipped to the South Pacific with the South Pacific Combat Air Transport Command. With rare exceptions his unit did remain out of the firing line. In 1944 he was sent back to the States and was in Washington again when the war ended.

At the suggestion of a Nixon family friend, he was invited back to California in 1946 to run on the Republican ticket for representative of the Twelfth Congressional District. Still in his naval uniform, he reported to Republican headquarters. His reserve, modest manners, and clean-cut appearance made an excellent impression. Under the guidance of veteran politician Murray Chotiner, he quickly mastered the stratagems of running for public office.

Nixon's campaign leaflets billed him as a forthright young American who had fought for his country "in the stinking mud and jungles of the Solomons"—a small lie, almost forgivable because it hurt no one. Less harmless, in that postwar period of hysteria, was the campaign itself, during which Nixon set out to convince voters that his Democratic opponent, Representative Jerry Voorhis, had Communist support. Vainly, Voorhis presented proof that Communists actually refused to support him.

As a novice congressman, Nixon got himself appointed to the House Committee on Un-American Activities, noted for its investigations of alleged "subversive activities." Nixon came to public attention in his investigation of Alger Hiss, president of the Carnegie Endowment for International Peace and a former government employee.

Whittaker Chambers, an ex-Communist turned informer, told the skeptical FBI that he and Hiss had stolen government secrets and given them to the Soviet Union. Nixon followed up on the story. Eventually Hiss was sent to jail not as a spy but for perjury; Hiss had said he did not know Chambers when in fact

Representative Richard M. Nixon (right)
conferring with members of the House
Un-American Activities Committee in 1948

he had known him under another name. Many felt that Nixon's performance was opportunistic. The criticism put him on the defensive; as his tapes would reveal, he never stopped describing and justifying his role in the Hiss case.

In his 1950 race for the Senate, Nixon again pinned the Communist label on his opponent, this time a woman. Helen Gahagan Douglas, wife of the actor Melvyn Douglas and protégé of Eleanor Roosevelt, had planned to devote her campaign to discussing California's mounting rural and urban problems. Instead she found herself caught in refuting Nixon's insinuations that "the pink lady" was "a tool of international communism." A weekly law journal came to Mrs. Douglas' defense and deplored the "whispered innuendos of Tricky Dick Nixon," giving him a nickname that stuck. Most California newspapers supported Nixon. No more than Voorhis did Mrs. Douglas have a chance to be judged on her ability for the job.

In 1952, when Nixon ran for Vice President on the ticket with Eisenhower, the New York *Post* exposed the existence of a secret Nixon fund, paid to him by seventy-five wealthy business executives who felt that he was "a fine salesman for free enterprise." As a result of the exposé, pressure was put on Nixon to resign. Eisenhower said reproachfully that he must be "clean as a hound's tooth."

Nixon took the offensive on television in his celebrated "Checkers speech." He had not taken any of the money of the fund for himself, he told his audience; every penny had gone for political expenses which he "did not think should be charged to the taxpayers of the United States." He talked about his wife, who did not have a mink but a "good Republican cloth coat." He went on to talk of a little dog named Checkers, which a Texas admirer had sent to his family and which he did not intend to return.

Nixon ended his speech with a plea for public support, which he did receive. There was no more talk of his withdrawing. Eisenhower and he were elected in 1952 and re-elected in 1956. As Vice President, Nixon achieved public notice particularly through incidents in foreign countries, such as his South American tour and his "kitchen debate" with Khrushchev.

In 1960, after eight years as Vice President, Nixon ran against John Kennedy for President, losing by a slender margin.

Two years later Nixon ran for governor of California against Democratic Governor Pat Brown. After his defeat, he angrily and resentfully told reporters that he was through with politics—that they would not have "Nixon to kick around" any more. Less well known than this outburst is his involvement in certain improper tactics during that campaign.

The California Democratic Council represented the liberal wing of the Democratic Party; they felt China should be admitted to the United Nations and called for a moratorium on nuclear testing. In a massive mailing of some 900,000 double postcards, Nixon attempted to win over conservative Democrats by deploring "the capture" of the Democratic Party by the CDC. Addressing the conservatives as "Dear Fellow Democrats," he advised them to refuse to vote for CDC candidates. Since the CDC supported the same candidates as the rest of the Democratic Party, this was tantamount to advising them not to vote for Governor Pat Brown. Nixon approved the text as did his campaign assistant, J. Walter Thompson advertising executive Bob Haldeman, later President Nixon's chief of staff.

By chance the Democrats found out about the postcards. Their attorney brought charges. The mailing broke state election laws since it did not include the address of the printer or the name of the sponsoring Republicans. It appeared to solicit money in the name of the Democratic Party without authority.

Vice President Richard M. Nixon (left)
with associate H. R. Haldeman in 1960

The case dragged on until 1964 and ended with a negotiated settlement. On record is the lengthy judgment of Judge Byron Arnold of October 30, 1964, in which he criticized both Nixon and Haldeman for improper conduct.

By this time Nixon had moved East and was working for a New York law firm, of which his future Attorney General, John Mitchell, became a partner. Nixon's law practice earned him considerable money and gave him the opportunity to continue his foreign travels and contacts with world leaders.

In 1968 he was back in the whirl of politics again, running against Hubert Humphrey for President. His unpleasant campaign practices of the past, which were part of the public record, did not keep the majority of American voters from deciding that Richard Nixon was the man they wanted for President of the United States.

The Cover-up
That Boomeranged

*"Remember the saying of Ennius,
'When crowns are at stake,
no friendship is sacred,
no faith shall be kept.'"*

*Marcus Tullius Cicero
(a favorite quotation
of Senator Sam Ervin)*

"Cover-up" is the word applied to the concerted effort on the part of the Nixon administration to conceal and deny any connection between it and the Watergate break-in. The earlier and most successful part of the cover-up paralleled Prosecutor Earl Silbert's investigation and interfered with it.

According to Jeb Magruder, there was never any question about the need of a cover-up. When word of the arrests reached the campaign committees and the White House, the cover-up was ushered in with "an orgy of paper shredding" of certain incriminating documents. At CRP, Gordon Liddy, not yet implicated, even shredded match covers which might have revealed the hotels where he had stayed. Magruder burned, in his living-room fireplace, Gemstone reports, including the transcripts of phone calls made by the Democrats. At the White House, John Dean emptied Howard Hunt's safe, but it was a week before he turned selected contents of it over to the FBI. Other materials he destroyed.

On June 18, the day after Watergate, John Mitchell, as head

of CRP, released a press statement that the man "identified as employed by our campaign committee"—he was referring to James McCord—ran his own private security agency, had his own clients, and had been employed months before by CRP to "assist with the installation of our security system." The statement was carefully worded to imply, without explicitly saying, that McCord had no present connection with CRP. The statement was typical of future administration half-truths about Watergate.

On the third day after Watergate, White House Press Secretary Ronald Ziegler told reporters that the White House would not comment on "a third-rate burglary attempt."

That same day, White House aide John Ehrlichman notified Patrick Gray, whom Nixon had appointed acting director of the FBI after J. Edgar Hoover's death, that Watergate matters were being handled by John Dean. Gray agreed to turn over FBI reports on Watergate findings to Dean, including raw data not yet checked and confirmed. Dean gave Gray two folders he had salvaged from Howard Hunt's safe, telling Gray they were "political dynamite." Gray obligingly took them home with him.

In a series of phone calls, Dean, Ehrlichman, and Haldeman urged Gray not to let his FBI agents probe too deeply into the $89,000 from Mexico deposited in Barker's Miami bank account —on the grounds it might embarrass the CIA. At the same time they told General Vernon Walters, deputy director of the CIA, another Nixon appointee, to stall any FBI investigation of the Mexican money. Walters, on July 6, rebelled against taking orders from "those kids in the White House" and assured Patrick Gray that the CIA was not involved in Mexico. Over the telephone, Gray told Nixon that members of his staff were trying to "mortally wound" him "by using the CIA and FBI. . . ." Nixon did not ask the names of those staff members, but told Gray to continue to pursue the investigation.

The White House aides also put pressure on Attorney General Richard Kleindienst, John Mitchell's replacement, and on Deputy Attorney General Henry Petersen to keep Watergate "isolated from the political element," that is, not to let Prosecutor Silbert dig too deeply into re-election campaign practices.

Thus, as an essential part of the cover-up strategy, the President's representatives were ordering around the FBI, CIA, and the Justice Department. "I think Nixon and his crowd thought they could get away with anything," historian Arthur M. Schlesinger, Jr., would say.

On June 22, 1972, five days after the break-in, Nixon held his first press conference since Watergate. A reporter asked him if he had made any investigation of Democratic Chairman O'Brien's charge that the people who "bugged" his headquarters had a direct link to the White House. Nixon said:

> *Mr. Ziegler and also Mr. Mitchell, speaking for the campaign committee, have responded to questions on this in great detail. They have stated my position and have also stated the facts accurately.*

Proof of Nixon's early involvement in the cover-up, produced over two years later, would force his resignation. This evidence was in the form of three taped conversations with Bob Haldeman, held June 23, the day after Nixon's press conference. In one of them, Nixon said:

> *. . . very bad to have this fellow Hunt, ah, he knows too much. . . . Just tell him to lay off.*

Other excerpts would prove not only that Nixon knew of the attempted manipulation of the CIA and the FBI but that he was the one who insisted on it.

On June 29, Maurice Stans, chairman of FCRP, turned over $75,000 in cash to Herbert W. Kalmbach, Nixon's personal attorney, the first installment of hush money paid to the Watergate Seven, who were also promised eventual clemency for their silence.

John Mitchell resigned as head of CRP on July 1, three days after the arrest of Gordon Liddy. FBI agents conducted interviews with CRP and FCRP employees; usually a CRP lawyer was present. One woman employee managed to get word to an FBI agent that she would like to speak to him privately. The next day her superior summoned her to ask what she wanted to tell the FBI. Employees were warned "to keep the ship together," which they knew meant that they should not tell anybody anything.

Nixon held another news conference on August 29. John Dean, he said, had conducted a thorough investigation of the Watergate break-in:

> *I can state categorically that his investigation indicates that no one in the White House staff, no one in this administration, presently employed, was involved in this very bizarre incident.... What really hurts in matters of this sort is not the fact that they occur, because over-zealous people in campaigns do things that are wrong. What really hurts is if you try to cover it up.*

Later, Dean testified that he knew nothing of the investigation he was supposed to have made at that time.

In a press conference on October 5, Nixon announced that the FBI had assigned 133 agents to Watergate, conducted 1,500 interviews, followed out 1,800 leads. He said:

> *I agree with the amount of effort that was put into it. I wanted every lead carried out to the end because I wanted to be sure that no man or woman in a position of major responsibility in the Committee for Re-election had anything to do with this kind of reprehensible activity.*

Step by step, he was being forced to back down from his original support of Ziegler's "third-rate burglary" statement. Explosions, like firecrackers ignited by Watergate, were going off all around him. The General Accounting Office, alerted by press stories, started investigating the campaign committee's financial policies and reported irregularities. On October 10, *The Washington Post* reported that the break-in was part of a huge campaign of political spying and sabotage directed by White House and CRP officials. Press Secretary Ziegler denounced the article as "the shoddiest type of journalism." But even after Nixon's landslide victory over Democratic candidate George McGovern on November 7, Watergate refused to go away.

The Watergate defendants became more demanding. "We're protecting the guys who are really responsible," said Howard Hunt in a taped telephone conversation to Charles Colson later that November, ". . . but at the same time, this is a two-way street and as I said before, we think that now is the time when a move should be made and surely the cheapest commodity available is money."

On February 28, 1973, the Senate Judiciary Committee held confirmation hearings on Patrick Gray's nomination as permanent FBI director. Gray freely admitted to the senators that he had sent FBI reports to John Dean and obliged White House aides in other unorthodox ways. Confirmation of his nomination was postponed and then dropped. Two months later, Patrick Gray made his most damning confession—that he had burned in his home incinerator the two folders of "political dynamite" that Dean had given him from Howard Hunt's safe. Gray was one of many whose careers were destroyed by Watergate.

According to numerous public statements from President Nixon, he first learned of the cover-up from John Dean on March 21, 1973. Tapes of that conversation give some evidence that what Dean said on that date was already known to Nixon. Nixon

Ex-presidential aides H. R. Haldeman (left)
and John Ehrlichman soon after their
joint resignations on April 30, 1973

discussed the question of further hush money for the defendants that same day with both Dean and Haldeman. Dean estimated the total would run to a million dollars. Nixon said:

We could get that. . . . If you need the money, I mean, uh, you could get the money. . . . What I mean is, you could . . . get a million dollars. And you could get it in cash. . . . I mean it's not easy, but it could be done.

Of Hunt's immediate demand for $120,000, he said, "Might as well . . . you've got to keep the cap on the bottle. . . ." And in another conversation, "For Christ's sake, get it."

The letter James McCord wrote to Judge Sirica on March 23—just two days later—threw the White House into a panic. There was worse to come.

On April 15, Assistant Attorney General Henry Petersen told Nixon that there might be enough evidence to warrant indicting Ehrlichman, Haldeman, and Dean on charges stemming from the Watergate cover-up. In a broadcast to the nation on April 30, Nixon announced the resignation of all three. He called Haldeman and Ehrlichman "two of the finest public servants it has been my privilege to know." He said nothing pleasant about Dean, who was already negotiating with the prosecutor for immunity in return for telling what he knew. Nixon also announced the resignation of Attorney General Richard Kleindienst; he had in fact withheld information connected with the break-in and later would be convicted of perjury in connection with the ITT scandal.

There could no longer be any doubt that the cover-up was weakening. Already it was a leaky umbrella. Soon it would become a sieve.

The Watergate Hearings

"The poorest man may in his
cottage bid defiance to all
the forces of the Crown.
It may be frail—its roof
may shake—the wind may
blow through it—the storm
may enter—but the king
of England cannot enter. . . ."

William Pitt, quoted by
Senator Herman Talmadge

At 10 A.M. on May 17, 1973, Senator Sam Ervin rapped his hand-carved gavel in the Senate Caucus Room to mark the opening of the Watergate Hearings, conducted by the Senate Select Committee on Presidential Campaign Activities, better known as the Ervin Committee or the Watergate Committee.

The six senators on the committee, besides Chairman Ervin of North Carolina, were Herman E. Talmadge, a Democrat from Georgia; Daniel K. Inouye, a Hawaii Democrat; Howard H. Baker, Jr., Republican of Tennessee and son-in-law of the late Senator Everett M. Dirksen; Edward J. Gurney, a Republican from Florida and Nixon's strongest supporter on the committee; Lowell P. Weicker, Jr., Republican of Connecticut, the only northerner; and Joseph M. Montoya, Democrat from New Mexico. Chief counsel was Samuel Dash, a Georgetown University law professor.

A blaze of klieg lights focused on the senators as Ervin made his opening remarks. The hearings were being televised, he said, so that the "full and open testimony" could heal the nation's wounds. Up to 25 million spectators listened to and watched the hearings in the next weeks, at least during their more exciting moments.

The television audience saw a succession of government employees and officials, nearly all of them male, all white, and all of respectable appearance. Yet these apparently solid citizens were being questioned about and sometimes confessing to, or involving others in, shoddy crimes.

James McCord, an early witness, described a thwarted plan of Howard Hunt to break into the office of a Las Vegas newspaper publisher, Hank Greenspun, allegedly to steal documents damaging to the Democratic candidates. According to Greenspun, they must have been after certain incriminating documents about millionaire Howard Hughes and the Justice Department. McCord also said that Jack Caulfield, a CRP undercover agent, had promised him not only money but a job and clemency "from the highest level" to keep silent.

Caulfield, a former policeman, admitted that with John Dean's authorization he had made that offer to McCord. He refused to implicate Nixon.

Another ex-policeman, Tony Ulasewicz, who looked something like Alfred Hitchcock but spoke with a New York accent, testified that he had delivered large sums of money to the defendants, their lawyers, or their families. He had received the money from Herbert W. Kalmbach, Nixon's personal lawyer. He made it clear that it was not an easy job to travel with a brown paper bag full of money, and to get it into the proper hands without detection. Ulasewicz furnished some of the few humorous moments of the hearings. In New York, he said, no one he knew would have bungled the Watergate job the way McCord and his friends had done. He added that the best way to get information about an opposition political party was to send a postcard asking for leaflets.

In the third week of hearings, Mrs. Sally J. Harmony, former secretary to Gordon Liddy, admitted typing memos for Liddy on forms headed "Gemstone," the code name for transcripts of the Democratic headquarters taps. Robert Reisner, former administrative assistant to Jeb Magruder, said that on Magruder's orders he had placed two Gemstone reports in a file Magruder took to a meeting with Mitchell. This was the first sworn testimony implicating Magruder and Mitchell in the bugging.

Hugh Sloan, who had quit his job as CRP treasurer rather than commit perjury, said that when he had large cash disbursements, such as those to Gordon Liddy, he asked Maurice Stans, head of FCRP, for his approval. Once when Sloan asked Stans what the money was for, Stans told him, "I do not want to know and you don't want to know."

Jeb Magruder, who had first perjured himself before investigators, had now decided to tell all. He said that he, Mitchell, Dean, and other higher-ups had approved the Watergate break-in, and went on to give details. Maurice Stans, prosperous, confident, distinguished, took the stand the fourth week of the hearings, and denied any "intentional violations of campaign financing laws." The senators were skeptical when he claimed that he gave $75,000 in cash to Nixon's lawyer, Kalmbach, without asking what it was for, and gave larger sums to Liddy in the same spirit of trust.

The first witness to bring Nixon into Watergate was John Dean. Having failed to gain immunity for himself, he still wanted to testify. His statement ran 245 pages. He described

John W. Dean III at the conclusion
of his testimony before the Senate
Watergate Committee in June 1973

meetings with Nixon in which the cover-up was discussed, quoted Nixon as saying that $1 million was not too much for hush money, spoke of Nixon's excessive concern with press leaks, his disregard for the law, his fascination with police intelligence, and his fear of demonstrations and dissenters. Dean also disclosed that Nixon kept an "Enemy List" of political opponents and almost everyone who criticized him.

John Mitchell, former Attorney General, former head of CRP, proved the most stubborn witness of all. He clung to the story that he had not authorized the break-in, and that he had kept information about the cover-up from Nixon so as not to interfere with his re-election. Chief Counsel Sam Dash said that in order to believe Mitchell's testimony the committee would have to disbelieve six other witnesses.

The unexpected climax of the hearings came on July 16, when Alexander P. Butterfield, deputy assistant to Nixon, revealed the existence of the presidential recording tapes. In the summer of 1970, he said, listening devices were installed in the Oval Office, in Nixon's other office in the Executive Office Building, in the Lincoln Room, and in the Aspen Cabin at Camp David. There was also a manual taping device in the Cabinet Room, which Butterfield turned on only when Nixon was present. The Secret Service had installed the devices and took care of changing the tapes, labeling them by date, and keeping them in storage. Haldeman knew about the system, but not Ehrlichman.

Thus everything the President said during his working hours, in interviews or over the phone, was recorded. So was the conversation of his visitors, including cabinet ministers and heads of states, without their knowledge or consent. Butterfield had been told that the purpose of the tapes was for a historic record.

In the next few days after Butterfield's revelation both the Watergate Committee and Special Prosecutor Archibald Cox, who was simultaneously investigating Watergate and related scandals, asked the White House for tapes in which Watergate affairs were discussed. Nixon refused to supply them. Subpoenas were issued to the President. This marked the launching of the "Battle of the Tapes," which was waged intensely for several months.

In the next days Nixon's lawyer, Herbert Kalmbach, admitted collecting money in cash for the defendants but claimed he thought it was for legal fees and family support only, not to buy their silence. John Ehrlichman took the stand and said, "I am here to refute every charge of illegal conduct." He blamed John Dean for the cover-up and everything else. He was followed by Haldeman, who was mild and respectful but pleaded a faulty memory to over 100 questions.

During the last week of the hearings, top executives or former executives of the CIA were called to testify. Richard Helms, former CIA director and presently ambassador to Iran, CIA deputy director General Vernon Walters, and former CIA deputy director General Robert E. Cushman in turn described the attempts of Nixon's aides to get them to hold up the FBI investigation of Watergate, to pay bail for the Watergate defendants, and to help Howard Hunt in pre-Watergate escapades, even to the point of supplying him with a red wig and other disguise paraphernalia.

The final witnesses at the hearings included Patrick Gray, Howard Hunt, and former Attorney General Kleindienst, who admitted to failing to report attempts of Dean and Ehrlichman to get him to ask for lenient sentences for the Watergate defendants.

The Watergate Hearings recessed on August 7, 1973, until

September. At that time their findings were released in a three-volume report, organized by subject matter with accompanying documentation, and with recommendations for legislation to prevent future Watergates. The report presented facts but did not pass judgment. To bring the guilty to trial was the task of Special Prosecutor Archibald Cox.

Abuses of Power
and Crimes
Against the Nation

*"I mean if you worked for someone,
he was God, and whatever
the orders were, you did it."*

*Hugh Sloan, describing
the atmosphere in
the Nixon administration*

Within a year after the Watergate break-in, scores of related scandals had been exposed. They encompassed breaking of the laws of the land and disregard of the Constitution, of the Bill of Rights, of the guaranteed privacy of individuals, of freedom of speech.

There were the widest abuses in FCRP, Maurice Stans' campaign finance committee. Stans was a genius at getting money. The over $50 million raised by the finance committee outdistanced by far any previous political campaign. Perhaps $20 million of this was in secret donations. Much of the money came from corporations; these were illegal contributions. Sometimes the donors were rewarded by a government favor, which was also illegal. The most generous givers were appointed as ambassadors in London, Paris, Austria, Trinidad, El Salvador, Jamaica, and elsewhere.

The milk industry was granted the right to raise the cost of milk after their donation. The carpet manufacturers were rewarded by the dropping of legislation requiring improved standards for testing flammable carpets.

The $89,000 "laundered" Mexican money had been part of a $100,000 gift by Robert H. Allen, president of Gulf Resources and Chemical Corporation. This was why the White House did not want the FBI to investigate the source of the money.

By federal law, after April 7, 1972, the sources of all large donations had to be identified. Up to that time contributors to FCRP who wanted their gifts kept secret could still safely deliver their gifts in cash. Although Nixon denied any role in soliciting campaign funds, his secretary, Rose Mary Woods, kept a list of all secret contributions.

According to Jeb Magruder, over $6 million in cash was collected in the last two days before the April 7 deadline. There was more afterward. The safe was stuffed with cash. Some of the staff persuaded trusted friends to keep large sums in their bank accounts. Over at the White House, attorney Kalmbach kept a large secret fund, part of which was left over from the 1968 campaign.

Nixon, who was greatly concerned with the need of internal security, employed Tom Charles Huston as an authority on radical student groups. In June 1970, Huston prepared a document on "Intelligence Gathering" that proposed increased electronic surveillance, opening of mail, surreptitious entry (burglary), and use of infiltrating agents on "violence-prone" campuses. Nixon approved the Huston plan but ostensibly abandoned it after FBI Director J. Edgar Hoover expressed distaste and disapproval. Later, the White House covertly put into action almost every phase of the Huston plan.

In May of 1969, *The New York Times* published an article on the secret bombing of neutral Cambodia which Nixon had authorized. Nixon thereupon ordered installation of seventeen wiretaps on thirteen government officials and four newsmen—to discover the source of the "leaks," he would claim. Seven of the taps were on employees of Henry Kissinger's National Security Council. One of them, Dr. Morton Halperin, left the government to campaign for Senator Edmund Muskie; the wiretaps were continued in his home. The American Civil Liberties Union brought a suit for Halperin against Kissinger; Kissinger's principal deputy, General Alexander Haig (a career army officer); Ehrlichman, and Mitchell (and later Nixon) for their attempts to monitor his political ideas.

In June 1971, Nixon approved the formation of the Plumbers, "a special investigations unit." Egil Krogh, John Ehrlichman, and David Young from the National Security Council were in charge. They set up quarters in Room 16 in the basement of the Executive Office Building, with a sign reading "The Plumbers" on the door. Charles Colson was liaison man with the White House. Howard Hunt and Gordon Liddy were among the Plumbers.

Nixon had been furious at the release of *The Pentagon Papers,* the official study of America's role in Vietnam, and vainly tried to keep *The New York Times* and other newspapers from publishing it. He asked the CIA and the FBI to prepare profiles of Daniel Ellsberg, who had admitted passing on the Pentagon material to the *Times.* Both profiles were favorable; the CIA said Ellsberg had acted from patriotism. Thereafter, John Ehrlichman approved a "covert operation" by the Plumbers to break into the Los Angeles office of Dr. Lewis Fielding, Ellsberg's psychiatrist, and steal Ellsberg's case history. Ehrlichman's approval had the notation "so long as it is not traceable to the White House." The mission was carried out by Hunt, Liddy, and several of their Cubans in September 1971; they failed to find the Ellsberg file.

Another undercover activity, known as the "Dirty Tricks" operation, was the sabotaging of Democratic presidential candidates. In charge of "Dirty Tricks" was Donald Segretti, hired by Dwight Chapin. Herbert Kalmbach paid Segretti over $45,000 from the White House secret fund. Segretti hired at least twenty-two agents for specific jobs.

During the primaries their special target was Senator Edmund Muskie, whose popularity rating in a 1971 poll was higher than Nixon's. In one incident during the Florida primaries a leaflet was distributed in Miami announcing a free lunch, free liquor, and a chance to meet Muskie and his wife at the Muskie campaign headquarters. The crowd of people who showed up were justifiably enraged to find the headquarters empty.

There were even more vicious Dirty Tricks, aimed at splitting the Democratic Party so badly it would destroy itself—such as a letter that went out on Muskie stationery falsely accusing Senator Henry Jackson of having an illegitimate daughter and saying that Hubert Humphrey had been arrested while taking a call girl out driving.

The Manchester, New Hampshire, *Union Leader* printed a letter, secretly written by a White House staff member, accusing Muskie of condoning slurs on Americans of French-Canadian descent, along with an editorial by the paper's right-wing publisher William Loeb criticizing Muskie. The next day *The Union Leader* ran an item falsely quoting Mrs. Muskie as saying to reporters, "Let's tell dirty jokes." It was too much for Senator Muskie, who broke down and wept publicly. His reaction is believed to have affected his fortune in the primaries.

After Senator George McGovern became the Democratic candidate, Dirty Tricks shifted over to his headquarters. The whole illegal, indecent, and often silly operation was fully exposed at the Watergate Hearings and Segretti was subsequently indicted and convicted. He was grieved and indignant.

Back in 1969, Nixon told his staff to get the Internal Revenue Service to stop tax exemptions to "leftist organizations." He considered anyone who opposed his policies an enemy. As John Dean testified, in June 1971, he had an Enemy List of twenty names drawn up, with a comment next to each name on a possible point of attack. Next to Morton Halperin's name was a notation: "A scandal would be most helpful here." A black congressman had the notation "Has known weakness for white females."

The list was later expanded to include several hundred names: organizations (Black Panthers, Common Cause, Farmers Union, SANE, Ralph Abernathy's Southern Christian Leadership Conference); labor leaders; over fifty newsmen, writers, and TV commentators; "political opponents," including Senator J. W. Fulbright, New York Mayor John Lindsay, Eugene McCarthy, eleven black congressmen and one congresswoman, Shirley Chisholm; celebrities, among them Carol Channing, Jane Fonda, Joe Namath, Gregory Peck, Barbra Streisand, Dick Gregory. Even some businessmen were on the list and certain businesses, such as a law firm of which former Attorney General Ramsey Clark was a partner, and the World Bank and its president, former Secretary of Defense Robert McNamara.

In connection with the list, John Dean drew up a memo, bluntly and crudely describing the subject as "how we can use the available federal machinery to screw our political enemies." One way to do this was to send their names in to the Internal Revenue Service. Harold J. Gibbons, a Teamsters Union official, Democratic National Chairman O'Brien, and *Newsday* reporter Robert W. Green were among several who were subject to IRS audits and investigations of their tax returns after getting on the Enemy List.

When news about this Enemy List was first made known to an incredulous public, there was a great deal of joking about it. In some circles it became a mark of prestige to have one's name included.

The Saturday Night Massacre

"Play it tough. That's
the way they play it
and that's the way we
are going to play it."

Richard Nixon to
H. R. Haldeman one week
after Watergate

On May 25, 1973, eight days after the Watergate Hearings opened, Elliot Richardson, veteran of three cabinet positions under Nixon, was sworn in as Attorney General, replacing Richard Kleindienst. At the same time the Senate Judiciary Committee confirmed Richardson's nominee for the post of Special Prosecutor, Archibald Cox, a Harvard Law School professor.

The task of the new Special Prosecutor was to continue and expand the Watergate investigations. He was given jurisdiction to investigate offenses involving the 1972 presidential election, allegations involving the President, the White House staff, and other persons appointed by the President. In getting testimony, Cox was granted the right to contest claims of "executive privilege." By law he could not be fired except for "extraordinary improprieties."

President Nixon approved Cox's appointment grudgingly and promised not to invoke executive privilege "as to any testimony concerning possible criminal conduct." Later he told Richardson that he had used the word "testimony" advisedly—to apply to oral testimony only, not to documents. About the same time Richardson received a phone call from John Ehrlichman telling him to make the Special Prosecutor keep away from national security matters. The odd thing about this call was that Ehrlichman was no longer on the White House staff and was under investigation himself.

In spite of this ominous beginning, Prosecutor Cox told friends that he expected to be at his job from three to seven years. He had a $2.8 million annual budget and gathered a staff of ninety employees. He could profit from the earlier work of Prosecutor Silbert and from the Watergate Hearings and had the cooperation of four men who were now talking freely: John Dean, Jeb Magruder, Herbert Kalmbach, and Frederick C. La-Rue, former assistant to Mitchell at CRP. While the Watergate Hearings were providing a public show, Cox was gathering material for indictments. In so doing, his investigations began to touch the White House.

On July 3, General Alexander Haig, who had replaced Haldeman as Nixon's chief of staff, called Richardson to convey Nixon's displeasure about an article in the Los Angeles *Times*. The article asserted that Cox was beginning an inquiry into the President's home at San Clemente, California. Cox was overstepping his bounds, said Haig, and would be fired if he did not "shape up." Cox denied that there was any formal inquiry under way on San Clemente, but he later announced that a review of the house purchase and improvements would be made by his staff.

When Cox learned about the existence of the presidential tapes, through Butterfield's revelation at the Watergate Hearings, he asked for tapes of nine conversations (five of which the

Ervin Committee had also demanded). Alan Wright, a Nixon lawyer, wrote that Nixon felt that to release the tapes would violate the "confidentiality" of the presidency. Henceforth Nixon often used that word "confidentiality."

On July 23, Cox issued a subpoena for the tapes. The subpoena was ignored. The case went to Judge Sirica, who ruled that Nixon should give the tapes to him, Sirica, and that he would then decide if they should go to Prosecutor Cox. Nixon defied the ruling. The case went to the U.S. Circuit Court of Appeals; on October 12 it ruled that Nixon must give the tapes to Sirica. This ruling came just two days after Vice President Spiro Agnew had been forced to resign to avoid prosecution for income tax evasion, and various charges of bribery against him were made part of the public record.

Nixon now moved against Cox. White House aides suggested to Elliot Richardson that he and Harry Petersen take over the Watergate investigation. "I wondered if I was the only sane man in the room or whether I was the one who was crazy," Richardson said later. He told the aides that the public would have no faith in such an investigation.

On October 19, Nixon offered to submit summaries of relevant parts of the tapes to Sirica and let Senator John Stennis of Mississippi (a long-time Nixon supporter and former judge) listen to the tapes and verify their authenticity—on condition that Prosecutor Cox agree not to ask for any more tapes or other records of Nixon's conversations. Cox turned down the Stennis plan.

The next day, Saturday, October 20, General Haig, speaking for Nixon, ordered Richardson to fire Cox. Richardson refused on the grounds that Cox had not by any standard committed "extraordinary improprieties"—and submitted his own resignation.

Haig demanded that Deputy Attorney General William Ruckelshaus, the next in line, do the firing. "Your commander-in-chief has given you an order," he told Ruckelshaus, revealing his military background. Ruckelshaus also refused and resigned instead. The next highest in the department, Solicitor General Robert Bork, was named Attorney General. On the advice of Richardson, who wanted him to stay on "and run the shop," Bork agreed to fire Cox.

The "Saturday Night Massacre," as the affair was called, brought more than a million letters and telegrams in the next ten days and perhaps two million more later. Most of them demanded Nixon's impeachment. Senator Edward Kennedy called the firing "a reckless act of desperation." Republicans as well as Democrats deplored the Massacre. Impeachment resolutions were introduced in Congress by Jerome Waldie of California and others. One of the few to defend Nixon was Gerald Ford, whom Nixon had just nominated Vice President.

On November 1, the beleaguered President appointed Leon Jaworski as the new Special Prosecutor. Jaworski, a Texas lawyer and former president of the American Bar Association, accepted on the condition that the White House would give him full cooperation and the independence he needed. He would prove no more willing than Archibald Cox to be controlled by the White House.

Nixon agreed to send the nine tapes to Judge Sirica, but it turned out two of them were missing. On a third, the crucial tape of June 20, 1972, made three days after Watergate, there was an eighteen-and-a-half-minute gap. Electronics experts would find that it was caused by deliberate erasures. The eighteen-and-a-half-minute gap exposed Nixon to ridicule. A joke spread through Washington: any secretary could get a White House job if she could erase a hundred words a minute.

The President's
Extras

*"It was not my habit to
interrogate the President
of the United States."*

*former Attorney General
Richard G. Kleindienst*

There were reasons why Nixon was so upset at the Los Angeles *Times* report about Prosecutor Cox investigating San Clemente, "the Western White House." Rumors about the President's lavish spending there were spreading. In May 1974, a House committee released a report criticizing the Secret Service, the General Services Administration, and presidential aides for permitting the spending of $17.1 million in government money on Nixon's vacation homes, mostly at San Clemente and Key Biscayne, Florida. The report called this "an extravagant expenditure for facilities used only a few weeks each year."

The expenditures broke down into $7.6 million for personnel (about $1.6 million a year); $5.6 million spent for communications; $2.2 million for "administrative support," and $1.7 million for protection. Of this last sum, something over $1.5 million was for permanent installations.

Since 1900 the Secret Service has protected American presidents. The Army installed fencing and alarm systems at President Eisenhower's Gettysburg home, along with guard booths converted from phone booths and other removable equipment, all at very little cost. President Kennedy had similar equipment installed by the Army at five separate locations. After Kennedy was assassinated, Congress granted the General Services Administration the authority to "provide lighting, guard booths and other removable facilities on private property" as an aid to Secret Service guards. Some $120,000 public money was spent on such expenditures on President Lyndon Johnson's private properties.

In the spending of public money, President Nixon outdid by far all his predecessors. Much of the work was in the form of major architectural and decorative additions. The procedure was for the Secret Service to present recommendations for needed installations to a presidential representative, usually Bob Haldeman or Herbert Kalmbach at San Clemente and Nixon's wealthy friend Bebe Rebozo at Key Biscayne. If Haldeman or Rebozo judged that a certain project was not "aesthetic," they would insist on revisions.

Typical was the case of the fence at Key Biscayne, for which the Secret Service showed a plan to Rebozo. In the name of the President, Rebozo vetoed the Secret Service model and said that Nixon wanted a fence like the one around the White House. It was built at a cost of $65,000—$20,000 more than the original estimate. At least one congressman later accused the Secret Service of not having the "guts" to resist Nixon's men.

Nixon did not care for guardhouses made over from phone booths, like those installed for Eisenhower; $50,000 was spent to construct custom-designed redwood and stucco guardhouses at San Clemente. Nixon's architect, Hal Lynch, purchased a Mexican lantern as a gate light and billed it to the GSA as "security related."

At San Clemente the GSA paid $13,500 for a new electric heating system, replaced rusty pipes and handrails, installed fire-

*A photograph taken from the air
showing the San Clemente complex*

fighting equipment. Government money also paid for furniture in Nixon's San Clemente den and an exhaust fan for his den fireplace, on the grounds that "downdrafts of smoke might cause the President's eyes to water." Flagpoles were installed at both residences.

At San Clemente alone more than $130,000 was spent on landscaping and landscape maintenance. According to the General Services Administration report, this meant restoring trees and shrubbery uprooted for the installation of security devices. Photographs taken before the work was done show only bare sand and underbrush. The GSA also provided full-time gardeners. A memo from John Ehrlichman suggested that a $40,000 annual contract for the San Clemente grounds be renewed at government expense.

Bebe Rebozo, Nixon's agent at Key Biscayne, is a Florida real estate dealer and banker. He came under investigation because of a $100,000 campaign donation from Howard Hughes which Rebozo claimed he kept in a safe-deposit box for over a year and then returned. The Watergate Committee did a massive investigation on the financial relationship between Rebozo and Nixon, too complex for this account. Among other curious facts, they found evidence that certain moneys turned over to Rebozo as campaign contributions were used to meet Nixon's personal expenses.

One item of $4,562, which originated as a campaign contribution, was passed by Rebozo through three bank accounts and a cashier's check, none in Rebozo's name. Following this devious journey, the money ended up as the major payment for a pair of platinum earrings set with eighteen pear-shaped diamonds and two tapered baguette diamonds. Nixon gave the earrings to his wife, Pat, for her birthday.

The taxes that Nixon paid on his income also drew public attention. As President, Nixon's salary was $200,000 per year. His investments brought in additional sums. He became a millionaire during his first term, but in 1969 he paid only $792.81 in federal income taxes. In 1970 he paid $878.03. His 1971 taxes were still under $1,000. One reason the taxes were so low was that he was taking a tax exemption of over $500,000 for papers accumulated during his vice presidency, to be donated to the National Archives. Before the Tax Reform Act of 1969, persons with valuable papers—writers, military men, government officials—were entitled to tax exemptions for material donated to libraries. The Reform Act limited these deductions to the "unappreciated value" of the material—little more than the cost of the paper. The White House succeeded in postponing the cutoff date of the new law to July 25, 1969. Even so, there was testimony that Nixon's gift had been backdated to get in under the deadline.

At least in part because of the press publicity, the Internal Revenue Service decided to re-examine Nixon's tax returns, beginning in 1969. A hand-delivered letter from the IRS reached Nixon on December 7, 1973, informing him of their decision. The next day Nixon wrote and made public a letter to the Joint Committee on Internal Revenue Taxation, authorizing them to examine his tax returns for 1969–72. Since he made no mention of the IRS letter, he gave the impression that he was the one who wanted the investigation.

The Internal Revenue Service subsequently rejected the entire deduction for the presidential papers. They found scores of other misrepresentations and nonallowable deductions—such as one of over $5,000 for his daughter's masked ball.

On April 2, 1974, the IRS, which the Nixon administration

tried to use so ruthlessly to punish its enemies, turned the tables. They disclosed that President and Mrs. Richard Nixon owed the sum of $432,787.13 in back taxes plus interest penalties of another $33,000. There was also a tax deficiency of $148,080.97 for 1969, which the Nixons had no legal obligation to pay.

It is just possible that the exposure of Nixon's income tax returns did more to shock the great mass of the American public than all the stories about the Watergate break-in, where after all nothing was stolen and no one was shot or killed.

The Press

*"Only a free and
unrestrained press can
effectively expose
deception in government."*

*Justice Hugo L. Black,
in support of the
Supreme Court's decision
in favor of* The
New York Times' *printing
of* The Pentagon Papers

Without the prodding and probing and detective work of American newspaper and news magazine reporters, the unraveling of the Watergate mystery would certainly have taken longer. Crucial portions might still be buried.

Three Pulitzer prizes were awarded to journalists for outstanding press coverage of Watergate. One of them went to *The Washington Post* for the work of two young and previously unknown reporters, Carl Bernstein and Bob Woodward. They tracked down Donald Segretti before his Dirty Tricks operation had come to light. They made dozens of other scoops. One of their sources for leads and confirmations was highly placed in the White House. The identity of this person, who detested what was going on, was known only to Woodward. They called him "Deep Throat" around the *Post* office. When people told Woodward and Bernstein they were spending too much time on Watergate, Deep Throat urged them to continue, saying they still had a long way to go to get to the bottom of things.

[49]

Because of their sleuthing, Nixon developed a special antipathy for *The Washington Post*. In one of the presidential tapes he is heard saying that the *Post* would have "damnable damnable problems." Subsequently two *Post*-owned radio stations in Miami and Jacksonville were singled out by four challenges to their license renewals with the Federal Comunications Commission; one of the challengers was a law partner of former Florida Senator George Smathers, an old friend of Nixon's.

Columnist Jack Anderson also won a place on the President's Enemy List by his pre-Watergate stories on the ITT scandal and on the $100,000 paid by Howard Hughes to Bebe Rebozo. One of his early scoops linked Bob Haldeman to the Watergate cover-up. The White House vainly tried to ferret out something unsavory about Anderson's past. Over at CRP, Jeb Magruder assigned Gordon Liddy to this chore. Liddy was no more successful than the White House had been.

James R. Polk of the Washington *Star-News* won a Pulitzer prize for his disclosure of dairy and trucking industry contributions to FCRP. Another Pulitzer went to Jack White of the Providence *Journal-Bulletin;* he broke the first important story about Nixon's amazing income tax returns. *The New York Times* was one of a number of newspapers that did excellent reporting on Watergate.

Though the majority of American newspapers had supported Nixon for President, as the Watergate scandals mounted Nixon was increasingly on the defensive toward the press. He seemed to have convinced himself that the news media were responsible for all his troubles. At the San Clemente press conference of August 22, 1973, one of his last, he was literally bombarded with embarrassing questions of a nature no President before him had had to face:

Why had he let Bob Haldeman listen to tapes refused to federal prosecutors and the public, at a time when Haldeman had resigned and was facing indictment? . . . When Patrick Gray, as acting director of the FBI, had warned him he was being mortally wounded by his aides, why did not Nixon ask who those aides were and what was going on? . . . The President had said that disclosure of the tapes could "jeopardize and cripple" the presidency. In face of such a risk, why had he made the tapes in the first place? . . .

The questions continued: The President had repeatedly said that he had tried to get all the facts about Watergate, yet John Mitchell had said that if Nixon had asked him about it, he would have told "the whole story chapter and verse." Was Mitchell speaking the truth?

The reporters asked him if he had tried to bribe the judge in the Ellsberg case, whether he himself had considered resigning, whether, if he were a congressman, he would not consider impeachment against a President who had authorized the Fielding burglary, mail surveillance, and other illegal acts. They asked him to substantiate his charge that people were exploiting Watergate to keep him from doing his job. They asked him why he had failed to turn over to the prosecutors information about criminal wrongdoing of members of his staff which he had received the previous March and April.

From long experience, the reporters who asked all these pertinent, impertinent questions knew that they probably would not get direct answers. That did not matter any more. What was important was to get everything on record, to let the people know the questions that stood unanswered.

The People

"If you once forfeit the
confidence of your fellow citizens,
you can never regain their
respect and esteem. It is true
that you may fool all the
people some of the time; you can
even fool some of the people
all the time; but you can't fool
all of the people all the time."

Abraham Lincoln

As the Watergate scandals escalated, there was a brisk sale of "Impeach Nixon" buttons, and others such as "Nixon Bugs Me" and "Don't Blame Me I Voted for McGovern." "Impeach Nixon" bumper stickers sold at fifty cents apiece. Others read: "Down with King Richard," "Visit San Clemente—You Paid For It." Smaller stickers sprouted: "Impeach Him Now More Than Ever."

All across the country peace groups and student organizations turned their energies to holding impeachment rallies, distributing impeachment leaflets, collecting signatures on impeachment petitions, encouraging people to press their congressmen to support impeachment.

Caroline Killeen, a former nun, bicycled from Florida to Waterloo, New York, in forty-three days, displaying an American flag and an "Impeach Nixon" sign.

An impeachment demonstration was held in Washington on April 27, 1974, attended by 10,000 people from thirty states. A

While campaigning for a local candidate in Michigan in April 1974, President Nixon seems to be ignoring the "impeach Nixon" signs.

huge banner bore the word "IMPEACH!" in great black letters; beneath it: "8 Million Indochinese Victims; Impoundment of Funds for Domestic Needs; Suppression of Civil Liberties; Illegal Secret Wars." The rally was followed by an Impeachment Fair, offering "Satire, Guerrilla Theatre, Puppetry & Soap-Boxing."

In front of the White House, demonstrators held up placards for passing motorists: "Honk if You Think He's Guilty."

Nixon supporters clung valiantly to the idea that his success in foreign policy outweighed his Watergate misdeeds. (Ironically, the visit to the People's Republic of China by Nixon, who had based his early career on anti-communism, had marked the zenith of his popularity.) But for many people, Nixon's diplomatic triumphs were offset by his support of the dictatorships in Greece and Portugal and America's role, through the CIA, in the overthrow of the Allende government of Chile.

As Watergate problems mounted, a grain sale was arranged with Russia. The deal drove up domestic grain prices and small farmers found themselves paying double or triple the former cost of their hogs' grain. The cost of bread climbed accordingly, as did that of beef, pork, chicken, sugar, and practically everything else. Inflation, which had been a slow-ebbing stream, turned into a raging torrent. With a Middle East embargo on oil, citizens of the American land of plenty waited in line for hours for gasoline. Unemployment increased. The stock market fell. Mortgage rates went into an upward spiral. Justly or unjustly, Nixon was blamed.

After the Saturday Night Massacre, a couple from Seattle, once loyal Nixonites, packed their children into their camper and drove East to Washington to present their petition for impeachment to Congress in person. A farmer in western New York State, stronghold of Republicanism, lamented, "And to think I voted for the SOB!" Congressmen were so swamped with letters from their constituents about impeachment that they had standard replies printed up. Protest was no longer limited to the young, the New Left, the minority groups. It was spreading among those whom Nixon had named the "Silent Majority."

The House
Judiciary Committee
Considers Impeachment
and the
Presidential Tapes

"No point is of more importance.
Shall any man be above Justice?
Above all shall that man be
above it who can commit
the most extensive injustice?"

George Mason of Virginia,
discussing the impeachment clause
of the Constitution at the
Constitutional Convention of 1787

Within two days after the Saturday Night Massacre, forty-four Watergate-related bills were introduced into the House of Representatives and eight impeachment resolutions were referred to the House Judiciary Committee. There had been earlier ones. Nine representatives—Conyers, Abzug, Chisholm, Ryan, Dellums, Rangel, Stokes, Mitchell, and Fauntroy—had introduced an impeachment resolution on May 18, 1972, a month before the Watergate break-in, mainly to induce the House Judiciary Committee to air certain charges against Nixon. Then soon after the Watergate Hearings opened, Congressman John Moss had moved to start impeachment proceedings; his proposal had been dismissed as premature. Most congressmen dreaded the thought of the cumbersome impeachment process, but after the Massacre it was obvious something had to be done.

The House Judiciary Committee began an inquiry into impeachment procedures about October 30, 1973. On February 6, 1974, the House of Representatives gave the Judiciary Committee authority to begin proceedings to determine whether or not there were sufficient grounds for the House to consider impeaching the President of the United States.

It was a solemn, awesome, agonizing moment in history.

Article II, Section 4, of the Constitution reads:

The President, Vice-President and all civil Officers of the United States, shall be removed from Office on Impeachment for, and Conviction of, Treason, Bribery, or other High Crimes and Misdemeanors.

To impeach does not mean to convict but merely to charge with misconduct in office. The House has the right to impeach an official by a majority vote. After impeachment the case goes to the Senate for trial. If the Senate finds the official guilty by a two-thirds vote, he is then subject to removal from office.

Impeachment has been rare. The House had voted for it only a dozen times. The only American President ever impeached, Andrew Johnson, was charged mainly with making speeches disrespectful of Congress and with firing his Secretary of War in violation of a new statute of doubtful constitutionality. He was acquitted when the Senate failed by one vote to get a two-thirds majority, and allowed to finish his term in office.

Now it all had to be gone through again.

Chairman of the House Judiciary Committee was Congressman Peter W. Rodino, a New Jersey Democrat and, like Judge Sirica, the son of an Italian immigrant. His committee had thirty-eight members—twenty-one Democrats and seventeen Republicans. As chief counsel, Rodino selected John Doar, a Republican who had served in the Justice Department. An unlimited budget made possible an impeachment staff of 105, nearly half of them lawyers. The staff was responsible for investigating the charges, assembling evidence, and studying the legal literature on impeachment. To avoid any danger of error, or any accusations of being partial, Rodino proceeded slowly and with caution—too slowly according to some.

Nixon's promised cooperation quickly evaporated. Through his Boston lawyer, James St. Clair, he excused himself from releasing White House material by pleading the "executive privilege" or "confidentiality of the presidency."

On April 11, the Judiciary Committee subpoenaed forty-two tapes it had first requested February 25. Nixon then made a surprise move. On April 29 he released 1,200 pages of tape transcripts of talks with his aides between September 15, 1972, and April 27, 1973. According to Nixon, they included all portions of the subpoenaed tapes relevant to Watergate. He offered to let Rodino and the senior Republican on the committee listen to the full tapes to determine for themselves whether the transcripts were accurate.

Several publishers rushed the transcripts into print in hardcover and paperback editions. Comparisons with the original tapes would later reveal that the transcripts had been heavily edited to put Nixon in a better light. Even as edited, they did him tremendous harm.

The Nixon of the transcripts seemed a vague and indecisive man, indifferent to world and domestic problems, interested only in saving his own skin, vulgar in his speech, even with all the "expletives deleted" from the transcripts. Haldeman

On April 29, 1974, President Nixon
released edited transcripts of the
tapes to the House Judiciary Committee.

showed Nixon scant respect, did not address him as "Mr. President" or "Sir," and interrupted him constantly. According to a report in *The New York Times*, anti-Semitic remarks and a reference to Judge Sirica as a "wop" had been deleted from the tapes. The President and his aides sounded more like gangsters than like responsible government officials.

The Republican Senate Minority Leader Hugh Scott summed up what many felt about the transcripts: "a deplorable, disgusting, shabby and immoral performance." Gerald Ford, the new Vice President, defended them, saying "the overwhelming weight of the evidence" proved the President "innocent of the charges." Ford was almost alone.

Nixon claimed, and seems in fact to have believed, that the edited transcripts would prove that he had known nothing about the cover-up before March 21, 1973 (nine months after the break-in), as he had insisted time and time again. Those who studied the transcripts carefully, to try and interpret the jargon in which they were couched, found hints and bits and pieces that indicated Nixon did know what was going on long before March 21 and that he had no scruples about the cover-up. This was confirmed by a revealing passage the Judiciary Committee found in the original tapes, omitted from Nixon's transcripts, of a March 22, 1973, conversation in which Nixon said to his aides:

> *I want you all to stonewall it, let them plead the Fifth Amendment, cover-up, or anything else, if it'll save it—save the whole plan.*

Was it possible that these instructions came from the same Nixon who had told the American people:

> *What really hurts [in matters of this sort] is if you try to cover it up.*

The Supreme Court Rules That a President Is Not Above the Law

*"Ever since World War 1
our government has been
increasingly lawless as it
caters to popular fears,
and indeed generates them
by cries of 'subversion'
and 'un-Americanism.'"*

*Supreme Court Justice
William O. Douglas
in* Go East, Young Man

The Nixon version of the presidential tapes did not satisfy Prosecutor Jaworski and Judge Sirica, any more than it had the House Judiciary Committee. In March a grand jury of the U.S. District Court in Washington had charged seven defendants—Mitchell; Haldeman; Ehrlichman; Charles Colson; Gordon Strachan, Haldeman's assistant; Robert Mardian; and Kenneth Parkinson—with conspiracy to defraud the government, to obstruct justice, and with other offenses. The grand jury named Nixon as an unindicted co-conspirator. (Colson later pleaded guilty to lesser charges, and was dropped from the conspiracy case. Strachan was granted a separate trial.) In connection with this case, Nixon was asked for sixty-four more tapes. He refused to surrender them. On May 24, 1974, Prosecutor Jaworski appealed to the Supreme Court to rule on whether the President could withhold evidence in a criminal trial.

Nixon had reason to think that the Supreme Court of 1974 would favor his point of view. Four of its nine members were now men appointed by him. A Republican, Chief Justice Warren E. Burger, had replaced Chief Justice Earl Warren, whose Court was responsible for the momentous school desegregation ruling of 1954.

Nixon had claimed he would fill all vacancies with "strict Constitutionalists," that is, judges who would interpret the Constitution literally. Indications are that he was more interested in appointments that would help him politically. Harry A. Blackmun was confirmed by a Congress which had rejected Nixon's first two choices, both Southerners, because of their lack of qualifications or past record. Lewis F. Powell was the one Democrat appointed by Nixon. The fourth Nixon appointee was William F. Rehnquist, who disqualified himself from the case, probably because he had served under John Mitchell in the Justice Department.

The two other Republican Supreme Court justices, Potter Stewart and William J. Brennan, were both appointed by Eisenhower. Byron White was a John Kennedy appointee. Thurgood Marshall had been selected by Lyndon Johnson. William Douglas, appointed by Roosevelt in 1939, was the oldest justice, and the one who had served the longest.

This was the texture of the Supreme Court now called on to pass judgment on the President of the United States in a case without precedent and of vital importance to the nation, because of its implications in regard to the delicate balance of powers between the judiciary and the executive branches of government.

Did the President have the power to withhold the sixty-four

tapes from the conspiracy trial on his claim that it was "not in the public interest" to release them? Did "executive privilege" properly apply to conversations that might have been part of a criminal conspiracy? The case of the United States of America *v.* Richard M. Nixon, President of the United States, was unique in another way: the President was facing the lawful challenge of a Special Prosecutor he had appointed.

For three hours on July 8, the Supreme Court listened to arguments presented in turn by Special Prosecutor Jaworski and Nixon's lawyer, James St. Clair. There were so many spectators that the 390 seats open to the public were rotated every five minutes. In the reserved section, Bob Haldeman, a defendant, sat next to Mrs. Jaworski, the prosecutor's wife.

Special Prosecutor Jaworski was the first to mount the lectern and address the eight black-robed justices. Speaking quietly and without histrionics, he made his most essential point:

> *Now, the President may be right in how he reads the Constitution. But he may also be wrong. If he is wrong, who is to tell him so? This nation's constitutional form of government is in serious jeopardy if the President, any President, is to say that the Constitution means what he says it does, and that there is no one, not even the Supreme Court, to tell him otherwise.*

It would be particularly inappropriate, Jaworski continued, to vest such power in President Nixon "in a personally delicate situation involving criminal charges against two of his closest aides and devotees [Ehrlichman and Haldeman]."

Next, lawyer St. Clair spoke brilliantly and with self-assurance. He belittled Jaworski's right to challenge the President, saying that "my brother," the Special Prosecutor, was part of the executive branch of the government. And the power of the executive branch was vested in the President. According to St. Clair, the President was the nation's chief law-enforcement official with final authority over whom to prosecute and with what evidence.

The President, commented Justice Stewart, "is submitting his position to the Court and asking us to agree with it."

Nixon did not contend he was above the law, St. Clair insisted, but that the only way the law could be applied to him was by impeachment.

But how could a President be impeached if he was able to conceal the evidence against himself? "You're on the prongs of a dilemma, huh?" Justice Thurgood Marshall said to St. Clair.

St. Clair murmured, "Very few things forever are hidden."

A large part of the session was taken up with nearly 350 questions from the justices, the most provocative directed to St. Clair. At one point Justice Marshall asked him how he could be certain that the subpoenaed tapes should be protected by privilege, since he admitted that he had not heard them. St. Clair said loyally that it was enough for him to know they were conversations between the President and his aides. There would come a time, very soon, when he realized that was not enough.

The eight justices met the next morning and discussed the case for six hours. They differed mainly in the degree to which they opposed the President. Chief Justice Burger prepared a draft which circulated among the other seven for the next two weeks. The result of their combined efforts was the thirty-one-page opinion which Burger read to the Court on July 24. In essence, it reasserted the Supreme Court's right to define the law.

Unanimously, they found that the President of the United States had no right to withhold evidence in criminal proceedings. Nixon was ordered forthwith to deliver the sixty-four subpoenaed tapes to Judge Sirica, so Sirica could decide if they were relevant for the conspiracy trial.

News of the 8 to 0 Supreme Court decision brought consternation to the White House. Chief of Staff General Haig waited forty minutes to tell Nixon. Seven hours later, St. Clair went on the air and announced that the President would obey the Court—but implied it would take time to sort the tapes. Prosecutor Jaworski was able to stop any more stalling with an order from Judge Sirica for St. Clair to begin delivery of the tapes that week.

The
Impeachment
Vote

*"The evidence convinces me that
my President has lied repeatedly.
Instead of cooperating with
prosecutors and investigators,
as he said publicly, he concealed
and covered up evidence, and
coached witnesses so that their
testimony would show things that
really were not true. . . . He praised
and rewarded those he knew had
committed perjury. . . ."*

*Lawrence Hogan, Republican
congressman from Maryland,
at a press conference
before the impeachment vote*

At 7:44 P.M. on Wednesday, July 24, just one half hour after
St. Clair announced that Nixon would abide by the Supreme
Court decision, the House Judiciary Committee began four days
of televised debate on the vast mound of evidence ("a sea of
material," one Republican congressman complained) which
Chief Counsel John Doar had assembled. The debate was a
spellbinding drama which gave Americans a unique behind-the-
scenes view of congressional proceedings. Chairman Rodino
opened the session, saying:

The Judiciary Committee has for seven months investigated whether or not the President has seriously abused power. . . . We have deliberated, we have been patient, we have been fair. . . .

Rodino himself had long been convinced that impeachment was warranted, but he was determined to try to avoid a strictly partisan committee vote of Democrats against Republicans. All of the thirty-eight members gave their views in opening statements. It became clear that, while judging the President of the United States had been an ordeal for all of them, the Republicans had suffered the most.

Charles Sandman, Republican of New Jersey, defended Nixon, saying that all of the witnesses had "testified no act of wrongdoing on the part of the President." David W. Dennis, Republican of Indiana, said, "I am shocked as anyone by the misdeeds of Watergate. . . . But I join in no political lynching where hard proof fails as to this President or to any other President." Charles Wiggins, Republican of California, said of the thirty-eight books of material that Doar had assembled, "My guess . . . you can put all of the admissible evidence in half of one book. Most of this . . . is not evidence and it may never surface in the Senate because it is not admissible evidence."

Lawrence Hogan of Maryland, Hamilton Fish of New York, Thomas Railsback of Illinois were among the Republicans who had wanted to believe in the President's innocence but who had been forced to change their minds. "It is suggested that we as politicians are all too tainted with corruption or moral imperfection to decide on the sins of Watergate," commented Fish. Walter Flowers, Democrat of Alabama, who had also favored Nixon, expressed his disillusionment:

If the trust of the people . . . is betrayed, if the people cannot know that their President is candid and truthful

*The House Judiciary Committee as
it opened debate, for only the second time
in U.S. history, on the possible impeachment
of a President, July 24, 1974*

with them, then I say the very basis of government is undermined. . . .

Even Democrats who had never favored Nixon showed a sense of betrayal. "This committee has heard evidence of governmental corruption unequaled in the history of the United States," said Jack Brooks of Texas. President Nixon's conduct in office, said Wisconsin Democrat Robert Kastenmeir, "is a case history of the abuse of presidential power." Elizabeth Holtzman of New York spoke of "a seamless web of misconduct so serious that it leaves me shaken." The erudite and eloquent Barbara Jordan of Texas said:

My faith in the Constitution is whole, it is complete, it is total, and I am not going to sit here and be an idle spectator to the diminution, the subversion, the destruction of the Constitution. . . .

To Robert Drinan, Democrat of Massachusetts, Nixon's most impeachable offense was concealment of the clandestine war in Cambodia:

There was, in my judgment, no justification for maintaining secrecy. . . . The Cambodians knew; the North Vietnamese knew; everyone knew except the people of America and this information was withheld from them until it happened to come out. . . .

The opening statements continued through most of Thursday. On Friday the floor was thrown open for debate. People watching TV were given the treat of hearing their representatives speaking extemporaneously, in accents ranging from the southern drawl, to the twang of the Midwest, to the clipped speech of the New Englanders. Sometimes there were sharp exchanges. The discussion was spiced with wit, bits of folklore. A motion to delay proceedings in the hope of getting the sixty-four tapes the Supreme Court had ordered Nixon to release was defeated. Voting on three Articles of Impeachment began on July 28.

The articles had been drawn up in long hours of painstaking labor in closed-door sessions. Each clause, each accusation was backed by pages of evidence from John Doar's "sea of material." Article I had to do with Nixon's involvement in the cover-up. It began:

> *In his conduct of the office of President of the United States, Richard M. Nixon, in violation of his constitutional oath faithfully to execute the office of President of the United States and, to the best of his ability, preserve, protect, and defend the Constitution of the United States, and in violation of his constitutional duty to take care that the laws be faithfully executed, has prevented, obstructed, and impeded the administration of Justice. . . .*

After the unlawful entry of the Democratic headquarters on June 17, 1972, the article continued, Nixon "using the powers of his high office, engaged personally and through his subordinates and agents . . . to delay, impede, and obstruct the investigation of such illegal entry. . . ." The next nine clauses of the article listed specific acts of the cover-up. The article ended (as did all three) with the words:

> *In all of this, Richard M. Nixon has acted in a manner contrary to his trust as President and subversive of constitutional government, to the great prejudice of the cause of law and justice and to the manifest injury of the people of the United States.*
>
> *Wherefore Richard M. Nixon, by such conduct, warrants impeachment and trial, and removal from office.*

The vote was taken by roll call of the committee members and was passed, 27 to 11. Six of those voting for the article were Republicans. Chairman Rodino was granted his wish. The voting was not on strictly partisan lines.

Article II dealt with Nixon's violation of civil rights and his misuse of government agencies. Clause (1) stated that "acting personally and through his subordinates and agents" he had endeavored to obtain confidential information from the Internal Revenue Service "in violation of the constitutional rights of citizens" and to cause "income tax audits or other income tax investigations . . . in a discriminatory manner."

Clause (2) had to do with Nixon's misuse of the FBI and the Secret Service. Clause (3) dealt with the Plumbers (though not by name): "a secret investigative unit within the office of the President, financed in part with money derived from campaign contributions, which unlawfully utilized the resources of the Central Intelligence Agency, engaged in covert and unlawful activities, and attempted to prejudice the constitutional right of an accused [Daniel Ellsberg] to a fair trial." The next two clauses gave more details of these accusations. Article II was carried by 28 votes, including 7 Republicans.

Article III focused on Nixon's violation of the law by refusing to deliver subpoenaed "papers and things." By his refusal, and "substituting his judgment as to what materials were necessary for the inquiry," Nixon had "interposed the powers of the presidency against the lawful subpoenas of the House of Representatives, thereby assuming to himself functions and judgments necessary to the exercise of the sole power of impeachment vested by the Constitution in the House of Representatives." This was the shortest of the articles and drew the least support: twenty-one members voted for it, including only two Republicans.

The committee also debated two other charges: Nixon's secret bombing of Cambodia without congressional approval, about which Congressman Drinan felt so strongly; and possible fraud in Nixon's income taxes. For a variety of reasons the vote went against recommending impeachment on either matter.

The work of the House Judiciary Committee was now over. The next step would be to present the case to the entire House. If the House voted impeachment, the case would go to the Senate for trial. All this meant more months of time-consuming effort, more expense.

Not all committee members were satisfied. Aside from a hard-core group of nine Republicans who voted against all three articles, there were others who felt that, in spite of the vast mound of evidence, something was still lacking. As one congressman put it, they needed "a smoking gun," the equivalent of a murder weapon, to prove their case irrefutably.

The
Smoking
Gun

"There is nothing covered,
that shall not be
revealed, neither hid,
that shall not be known."

The Bible,
King James version

There was a great deal of speculation as to whether the President would comply with the Supreme Court order and turn over the tapes in question. His lawyer, St. Clair, announced that he intended to do so. On August 5, 1974, Nixon released three of the sixty-four tapes, containing conversations between him and Haldeman, made on June 23, six days after Watergate. In so doing he delivered the "smoking gun" that had been missing.

The June 23 tapes showed, beyond all doubt, that Nixon was responsible for the attempt to get the CIA to keep the FBI from following up crucial clues.

At one point Haldeman tells the President:

Now, on the investigation, you know the Democratic break-in thing, we're back in the problem area because the FBI is not under control, because Gray doesn't exactly know how to control it and they have—their investigation is now leading into some productive areas—because they've been able to trace the money—not through the money it-

self—but through the bank sources—the banker. And, and it goes in some directions we don't want it to go. . . .

The President says, "That's right."
Haldeman continues:

That the way to handle this now is for us to have Walters [General Vernon Walters, deputy director, CIA] call Pat Gray and just say, "Stay to hell out of this—this is ah, business here we don't want you to go any further on it." That's not an unusual development, and ah, that would take care of it.

The President asks, "What about Pat Gray—you mean Pat Gray doesn't want to?" Haldeman tells him, "Pat does want to. He doesn't know how to. . . ."
In another passage, Nixon talks of Howard Hunt:

Of course, this Hunt, that will uncover a lot of things. You open that scab there's a hell of a lot of things and we just feel that it would be very detrimental to have this thing go any further. This involves these Cubans, Hunt and a lot of hanky-panky that we have nothing to do with ourselves. Well what the hell, did Mitchell know about this?

"I think so," Haldeman tells him.
The President continues:

He didn't know how it was going to be handled though— with Dahlberg and the Texans and so forth? Well who was the [expletive deleted—Ed.] that did? Is it Liddy? Is that the fellow? He must be a little nuts.

"He is," says Haldeman. The President continues, "I mean he just isn't well screwed on is he?"

This conversation took place five days before the FBI picked up Gordon Liddy, through their own detection, not because Nixon or any of his staff informed them of his connection with the break-in. It is a crime to withhold information about someone involved in a crime.

In a public statement that was released at the same time as the three tapes, Nixon said that he had listened to them back in May and recognized that they "presented potential problems," but that he had not informed his staff, or his counsel (St. Clair), or those arguing his case, "nor did I amend my submission to the Judiciary Committee." He admitted that "this was a serious act of omission for which I take full responsibility and which I deeply regret." He realized that "portions of the tapes . . . are at variance with certain of my previous statements."

This was the nearest that Nixon ever came to admitting that he had not always told the truth about Watergate.

It seems to have been James St. Clair who, hearing the tapes for the first time and being perhaps indignant that any client of his would keep such pertinent information from his lawyer, persuaded Nixon that he must make this public admission of guilt. After Nixon agreed, Patrick J. Buchanan and Raymond K. Price, Jr., two of his speech writers, spent five hours composing his statement to try to make it sound less damning than it was.

"We knew it would be devastating," Price said later.

On August 2, three days before Nixon released the statement, St. Clair asked Republican Congressman Charles E. Wiggins, a well-respected attorney and the strongest pro-Nixon voice on the House Judiciary Committee, to come to the White House. St. Clair and General Haig showed him the transcripts. Wiggins read them unhappily. To the end he had insisted there was no direct evidence to prove Nixon's involvement in the cover-up. Reluctantly he said now that it would be "wholly appropriate to consider the resignation of the President." The eight other House Judiciary Committee Republicans who had voted against impeachment subsequently read the transcripts with sorrow and dismay. After that Nixon's statement was released to the press, causing shock waves across the nation.

Newspapers were publishing stories to the effect that if Nixon resigned he would get an annual pension of $65,000 whereas if he were impeached he would get nothing.

Eight Republican senators, including the liberal Jacob K. Javits of New York and the conservative Barry Goldwater of Arizona, met with Nixon on August 7. Goldwater went over, one by one, the names of those who might just possibly vote for Nixon during the impeachment proceedings—perhaps fifty in the House when 218 were needed to prevent impeachment; perhaps fifteen votes in the Senate when Nixon needed thirty-four to get an acquittal.

Senator Hugh Scott said that the situation was gloomy. Goldwater called it hopeless. After the meeting, Nixon told his family he would likely resign. His daughter Tricia wept.

The next evening he gave his resignation speech to the nation. His manner was remarkably controlled. All the humiliations that had been heaped on him in the past months—the half-million tax payment the IRS demanded, the impeachment vote, the Supreme Court decision, the stream of over forty of his close associates who were indicted or arrested or in prison, the formerly loyal colleagues who now condemned him—none of this had apparently changed him. He admitted to mistakes but not to misconduct. He emphasized what he considered the outstanding accomplishments of his presidency, especially his foreign policy initiatives.

The next morning, August 9, Secretary of State Henry Kissinger received a short note:

Dear Mr. Secretary:
I hereby resign the office of
President of the United States.
Sincerely
(signed) *Richard Nixon*

At that moment Gerald Ford became President.

An almost audible sigh of relief swept the land, and with it an onrush of patriotic pride. The unprecedented change in government had been made without bloodshed and without violence. The two-hundred-year-old Constitution had worked. The wisdom of the separation of powers—the executive, the judicial, and the legislative—had been proven. With all the delays, the costly procedures, the occasional errors of the investigative bodies, democracy had worked. A free press and a basically independent people had all helped. Congress had acquired a new dignity.

Aftermath

*"Our country will
survive this tragedy."*

*the late Chief Justice
Earl Warren,
during his last illness*

The United States seemed to come back in focus with the inauguration of President Gerald Ford. Ours was no longer a land where people had their telephones tapped, their mail read, the privacy of their homes threatened, where the men at the top compiled enemy lists and sought revenge on political opponents, student rebels, crusading journalists, and anyone else who happened to cross them. We were, so it seemed, once again part of a sane and normal world.

There was a party at the White House; everyone danced and had a good time, including President Ford and his wife. There was something very pleasing about President Ford's simple unassuming manners and his pledge of an open government.

Then on September 8, one day short of a month after he took office, President Ford announced "a full, free and absolute pardon" for Richard Nixon. Ford's pardon of Nixon broke the spell of well-being. Watergate was back on the front pages in all its horror. The country was once more split. Was the pardon really just "an act of mercy," as Ford insisted? Or was it the old political custom of a favor for a favor?

The first reaction was in the White House, where J. F. ter

Horst, Ford's press secretary, resigned in protest. *The New York Times* called the pardon "an act of monumental folly that insured the cover-up of a cover-up" and "subverted the spirit of the law and the Constitution." The general consensus was that after all the American people had been through, they had the right to know the truth and the whole truth, as only a full-scale trial could reveal it, and that they were now deprived of that right.

In Judge Sirica's court, the five men indicted for cover-up activities at once demanded an indefinite delay of their impending trial. If the former President, for whom they were in such grave trouble, and whom the grand jury had named as an "unindicted co-conspirator," could be pardoned, were they not entitled to the same consideration?

Their demand was denied. On January 1, 1975, after a sixty-four day trial, a jury of nine women and three men reached a verdict. Mitchell, Haldeman, and Ehrlichman were all convicted of conspiracy to obstruct justice, of obstruction of justice, and of various counts of perjury. Mitchell and Haldeman faced possible sentences of up to twenty-five years; Ehrlichman, twenty years, maximum. Robert Mardian was convicted of a single count of conspiracy to obstruct justice, facing a possible five years in prison. All four, still free, made immediate plans to appeal the verdicts. Only Kenneth Parkinson, a former Nixon campaign committee lawyer, was acquitted.

The most dramatic parts of this long trial had been the playing of presidential tapes, not previously released, giving more proof that Nixon was the mastermind of the cover-up. Because of the pardon granted him by President Ford, Nixon could not be prosecuted for his actions, in spite of the public protest that had broken out against the pardon.

A bitter lesson had been learned. Watergate was not actually the fault of Richard Nixon. Watergate was the fault of the American citizenry who, ignoring what should have been plain, voted him to power. Engrossed in their own affairs, the older generation had failed to keep that eternal vigilance that is the price of liberty.

Will the young, who have been brought up on Watergate and know its perils, do better than their elders?

Bibliography

Anderson, Jack, with Clifford, George. *The Anderson Papers*. New York: Ballantine Books, 1974.

Berger, Raoul. *Impeachment: The Constitutional Problems*. New York: Bantam Books, Inc., with Harvard University Press, 1974.

Bernstein, Carl, and Woodward, Bob. *All the President's Men*. New York: Simon & Schuster, 1974.

Chidsey, Donald Barr. *The Birth of the Constitution*. New York: Crown Publishers, Inc., 1964.

Costello, William. *The Facts About Nixon*. New York: The Viking Press, Inc., 1960.

Dobrover, William A.; Gebhardt, Joseph D.; Buffone, Samuel J.; and Oakes, Andra N. *The Offenses of Richard M. Nixon*. New York: Quadrangle/The New York Times, 1974.

Evans, Rowland, and Novak, Robert D. *Nixon in the White House*. New York: Random House, 1971.

The Impeachment Report. A Guide to Congressional Proceedings in the Case of Richard M. Nixon, President of the United States. New York: New American Library, 1974.

Magruder, Jeb Stuart. *An American Life: One Man's Road to Watergate*. New York: Atheneum, 1974.

Mankiewicz, Frank. *Perfectly Clear, Nixon from Whittier to Watergate*. New York: Popular Library, 1973.

Mazo, Earl, and Hess, Stephen. *Nixon: A Political Portrait*. New York: Harper & Row, 1967.

The New York Times. *The End of a Presidency*. New York: Bantam Books, Inc., 1974.

The New York Times. *The Watergate Hearings*. New York: Bantam Books, Inc., 1974.

Osborne, John. *The Nixon Watch*. New York: Liveright Publishing Corporation, 1970.

The Senate Watergate Report. Introduction by Daniel Schoor of CBS. New York: Dell Publishing Co., Inc., 1974. 2 volumes.

Sussman, Barry. *The Great Coverup: Nixon and the Scandal of Watergate.* New York: New American Library, 1974.

Vidal, Gore. *An Evening with Richard Nixon.* New York: Random House, 1972.

Washington Post, staff of. *The Fall of a President.* New York: Dell Publishing Co., Inc., 1974.

Washington Post Commentary. *The Presidential Transcripts. The Complete Transcripts of the Nixon Tapes.* New York: Dell Publishing Co., Inc., 1974.

Wills, Garry. *Nixon Agonistes.* Boston: Houghton Mifflin Company, 1970.

Index

Watergate Hotel. *See* Watergate scandal
—break-in
Watergate scandal
  break-in, 3–11, 48, 56
  committee, 26–32, 40, 41, 43–48
  cover-up, 19–25, 50
  hearings, 26–32, 40, 41
  Nixon involvement. *See* Nixon, Richard Milhous
  press involvement in, 49–51
  public reaction to, 52–56
  Senate report on, 9
  Supreme Court involvement, 61–65, 66, 70, 73

Weicker, Lowell P., Jr. *See* Watergate scandal—hearings
White, Byron, 62
Wiggins, Charles, 67, 75
Wills, Frank, 3
Woods, Rose Mary. *See* Abuses of power charges
Woodward, Bob, 6
  See also Press involvement in Watergate
Wright, Alan, 41

Young, David, 35

Ziegler, Ronald, 20, 21, 23